The
Necessity
of
Ashes

FELICIA D. BULGOZDY

Artellectual Media LLC

ISBN: 979-8-9993570-1-4 (Hardcover)
ISBN: 979-8-9993570-0-7 (Paperback)

Printed in the United States of America.

Artellectual Media LLC
7821 Saint Andrews Road
PO Box 375
Irmo, S.C. 29063

www.Feliciad.com

For anyone in search of something…
be it your life,
your love,
or your people.

When it finds you,
I hope it's more wonderful
than you could have ever imagined.

1

2

3

4

5

Me: I made it.

Her: Made what?

Me: The list.

Her: Let me see it...

...

Her: (chuckling)

Me: What?!?

Her: That's cute. Don't worry...
it'll change.

Me: Why do you say that?

Her: (smiling) You'll see...

PART 1

GLIMPSES

Glimpses of you
have got me vibing like
a fifteen year old admiring the
            poly-rhythmic tracks laid over the
        soft rush of the wind laid over the
    smooth melodies on the radio that perfectly compliment the
            grey skies of a
                rainy Saturday morning...

        with windows open...

                and nowhere to go.

I'm lying here,
leisurely listening,
loving the lingering fragrance
of your simple,
yet luxurious
                            fresh rain.

My heart pounds as I'm
lying in bed dreaming of the you
that I thought I knew
when I thought I knew you
by some other name.

I can recall a glimpse of you
in one's smile,
in another's resolve, and even
in someone else's insecurities.

I've seen you
in their various statuesque silhouettes,
in maneuvers that let me know that your mama
"raised you right".

Glimpses of you
are in the pictures
that lyrics on the radio
paint in my mind...

How
"I could drink a case of you..."
and still be up for more.

You call me in their melodies.

In my mind's eye,
I've watched us move together,
swaying slowly,
wrapped,
willingly trapped,
and entangled in each other's embrace
as we dare to let each other become our
"One and only".

I've heard you,
through the booming bass of their voices,
send my spine quaking because
you, sir,
have disturbed my fault line.
The sheer reverberation of your timbre
commands my attention...
and you have it.

My eyes then search for you.

They wander.

They scan.

But despite my best efforts...

                        I've only caught glimpses of you.

I've seen you
in those called by other names,
some even impersonating you,
but
proving to be caricatures,
imitating and exaggerating
the features that are
only
organically
yours.

                        How I long to know your real name.

You see,
I can sense your essence and it's
different.
It's sweet;
warm and kind,
unashamed and...
determined.
Your gentleness is ever present,
and your wrath has but one boundary
to encapsulate it...
me.

I sometimes find myself struggling to remember
that the others I've seen are not you,
are not the original,
but a variation of your melody,
or a sample of your song,
or just…

                                                    a cover.

They appear
their gestures glutted with romance,
as if to prove to me that they are
somehow
                              "different"
somehow,
                              "the one."

They aim to be chosen
for a while
by convincing me that
no one else has ever
                              "made me feel…",
all the while having no clue what
                              "makes me feel…"
and not caring enough to ask.

They don't realize
that your portrait,
while not yet crystal clear to me,
is unmistakable,
so no one will be able to just...

                                                    pass.

It won't only matter that I'll know you...
because you'll know me.

Still
I've seen glimpses of you
in those who "saw" me

                                        but didn't...
in those who "valued" me

                                        but couldn't.
They told me
        "You're so smart",

                        so "beautiful",

                so "talented",

                                so "good to me"...
and then held my hand
only long enough to realize that
I was a variation on the melody
that they
really longed to hear.

9

They found themselves having to admit that
I was merely a caricature
of the one
that they
really wanted,

that something was missing for them too,
and that all the while
they'd been pretending
that I was...

"That girl."

But you,

you knew.

Because you've been seeing your own glimpses of me,
encountering your own caricatures,
and you refused to settle.

You've been looking
for me
just like I've been looking
for you.

And because of this,
no one else will ever do.

My List... age 18

What I want in a guy...
- have green eyes/brown hair
- be tall
- play guitar
- be a Christian
- want lots of kids
- currently have no kids
- have a college degree
- be really smart
- dress well
- be faithful to me

Me: Have you ever dreamt of a feeling?

Her: What do you mean?

Me: Like... you can sense something... but you don't know why?

Her: No.

Me: Well, I had the craziest dream last night...

S O L A C E

Rolling over, I encountered it all.

It was a sense of ecstasy
that I could barely comprehend...
the divine oscillation of my spirit
in the sweet pendulum that was you.

There.
You were there... and so was I.

Enveloped in a peace
that could only be commanded
by the One to whom all power belongs,
I felt your exhale,
and then an extension,
a reach,
disturbing the warm, tender cradle
that I had so willingly melted into.

Then came my obvious response.

Being prompted by your soft shift,
I was probed to turn,
so that I might confirm
the source of the elation I had been experiencing...
That yours was the form
that my form had been conforming to
for what seemed like
hours.

But when my slumber was finally broken,
you were gone.

All that remained was the peace,
the confirmation that you were there with me,
that you'd be back again someday...

and that in those moments,
I felt an entire lifetime
of what's to come.

Me: *sigh*...I know, I know. I'm romanticizing it. I hate how that's so easy to do now that he's gone. He wasn't even the one in my dream.

Her: How do you know it wasn't him...?

Me: I just know... but I still miss him.

Her: You know your mind is playing tricks on you. The truth is that you two weren't good for each other.

Me: I guess hindsight is 20/20... eventually. Until then...

PART 2

EXODUS

Where did this begin?

This feeling is no stranger to denial.
They've lived together for years now,
but this feeling is making a gallant attempt
at a triumphant return,
and I need to cut it off at the pass.

Right now.

Maybe then perhaps I can find the origin,
cut off the air supply,
and suffocate it.

I've been searching for years now,
hoping to finally locate my heart
within a theory
where I can place our tragedy.

A theory backed by my research of past loves,
triangulated with the impromptu interviews
of those who possess similar battle scars
and the constant observation of you...
My "n" of one.

You keep turning up here.
but If I can find that place,
then maybe I can just nip,
tuck,
chip,
and slash away at its foundation,
instead of my own sanity
...this time.

If I can avoid the implantation of another "us"
rather than abort it
post-conception,
then perhaps I can remain whole
by gladly trading miscarriage
for no carriage at all.

You see, I've lived on this block my whole life
and every now and then,
I wander this block several times over,
just to prove to myself that it's still mine...
that you've vacated...
that you're never coming back.
I witnessed it the first time,
and the second,
and the third,
and... *sigh*... never again.

So then I guess it's good for me to go back,
yet again,
just to make sure that you're not trying to
"... find a place to turn into..."
even if its only for a little while.

Diligently, I scurry over my chosen territory
in search of our next possible initiation,
the weakest link,
the smallest crevice,
where we could begin again.

I wander around my block,
walking slowly past the places
where my memory serves sweet recollections...
our memorials...

      ... smiles...

         ... blushing...

            ... a taste in the darkness at midnight,

and me engulfed in your aura.

I slow down even further to catch a whiff
of your chemistry.
It's one so unique that
even Coco Chanel couldn't duplicate it
and if she could,
I'd go broke trying to experience it
just one more time.

On the buildings, there are billboards,
portraits of you that showcase
those crystal pools of sky,
that would send my heart into flurries
upon each and every meeting with my own.

They always were your best feature.

Then there was the soft fuzz
that hinted to me the hour
for quite some time.
Now I settle for a wristwatch.

Five o'clock looked better back then...
on you.

I round the corner to take in the grandeur
of an old oak,
its statuesque figure towering over me,
draping over my property,
a work of art with grace unmatched,
its wisdom dripping like honey from its branches.
Every time the crisp wind blows
his limbs offer strength, a comfortable seat,
and a listening ear.

He's your twin.

No wonder why you lived here.
No wonder why I loved you so.

The wind disturbing everything in its presence
sweetly embraces me for just a second
before finding its way into a gathering of leaves
that creates a whirlwind on the ground
and then fall motionless soon after...

Much the way your arms have done.

There it goes again.

This time the sound of the wind rises,
rushing through the only instruments it can find,
the lonely trees and vacant houses,
like the air I used to await at the end of your horn.

Its mission is different now.
The melody is still beautiful
but even in its beauty,
it is more somber,
surreal,
sweet, but in a different way.
Perhaps it is because I know that
it's the only one that will ever be played for me now.

I stand there for a moment,
addicted,
listening to the remnants of you,
not wanting to move,
dying to hear more,
and falling apart
note by note.

Then, mustering up the strength to finally leave,
or maybe just realizing that I'm slitting my own wrists,
I round the next corner.

Oh God,

This is where it happened.

I want to run, but running would be my admission

that I am afraid of a place that I supposedly own.

So to save face,

I walk.

This is my property.

I dare not comb the dilapidated buildings with my

magnifying glass

in search of any signs of life in the rubble

for fear of new wounds,

and re-opening old ones.

I am amazed at how it still feels like a fresh demolition

even after all this time,

with no vegetation peaking through the floors,

qualifying the ruins to be labeled artistic and unique

by having acquired their beauty with time.

Here, there is no hope,

no sign of forgiveness,

no recompense,

no...

Nothing.

So I walk.

I walk right past the past...

                    more briskly past the "right"...

and then the "wrong"....

                        away from the "why"...

       and even beyond our "I don't knows".

I shed a tear for our stubbornness
and I want to scream out every word that I've never said,
that I'd been dying to tell you
since we met,
we loved,
and we were done.

At the end of the block
I look back one last time,
straining to hear anything that can be said
to make it better,
to make me shed
one
less
tear.

                        Nothing.

At last...
the side of the street where I currently reside.
I'm exhausted but
I'm home.

My house is secure and charming,
and to circumvent the eerie feeling of loneliness,
I occupy all the rooms myself,
with...

                                    myself.

You have no billboards here
and the doors keep me from experiencing
the chill of your wind.
Our mausoleum is blocked by Dogwoods and
Magnolias.
I planted them myself.
In a few years they may actually block my view,
but until then
I'm determined to pretend.

I've been wandering so long today
that I now have to recall why I went...

...Oh...

    ...yeah...

to find place where it could all start over...
to avoid this flood of emotion
that by which I am currently subdued.

Then,
gazing out of my window,
tucked away from the happiness that you bring
and the pain of your absenteeism,
I realize where it is...

It used to be mine.
but somewhere between
my reminiscing of who you were
and my recollection of how we failed,
you still dwell on my block.

Your fondest accounts are still in my back yard
and you still inhabit my mind,
with an absence that seems almost larger
than your presence.

No matter where you are
or what we do,
the block is ours,
as is the story,
and the tragedy is doomed to transform and replicate itself
every time I go in search of the beginning
to end it,

because I know now that the next beginning...

       ...has just begun within me...

          like it has every time before.

And I've fallen for you once again.

My List... age 23... edit #4

What I want in a guy...
- have green eyes/brown hair
- be tall
- ~~play guitar~~ be a musician
- be a Christian + respectful of other's beliefs
- want lots of kids
- currently have no kids
- have a college degree
- be really smart
- dress well
- be faithful to me
- dance salsa
- be confident
- be charismatic
- have a beard ???
- values my opinion

Me: I guess I just feel like I'll always be "the single friend". At least you've had the experience of actually dating. I always get close and then it falls apart.

Her: It's not really that great.

Me: I know but still... I'd love to have an actual boyfriend for once. No "will they, won't they" crap... one that I feel is worth all the trouble.

Her: Girl, are you sure you want that kind of trouble?

SAILING

Circumstances had me shipwrecked on the island,
the land that I...

"loved".

I lived on the coconuts there,
using their sugary nectar,
as cloyingly sweet as it was,
numerous times
to try to quench my thirst,
illuminating my hair with their oils,
and dining on their meat.

As I gloried in this supposed bliss
And raved about their flavor,
I knew all the while

that their flavor activated my gag reflex.

I hated the way they tasted.

I believe that the island was poured for me,
by me.

Deep within the murky depths of the
seemingly glistening waters of my life,
that first grain of sand
laid the foundation of this residence,
the very moment I realized
who they were in my eyes,

                and who in their eyes
                  I would never be.

Every tear,

      insult,

         and act of disregard

            accumulated

              somewhere deep

                within the core

                  of me.

Miserable memories loved company
and they found plenty,
until there were enough of them
to collectively form the sandy mountain
on which I've stood for some time now.

My consciousness,
after doggedly navigating experience after experience,
was worn,
blinded by tears,
and shipwrecked on an isle
that had been built
by the disappointments of former days.

It was hot there,
with no company
and no real companionship to speak of.

So I paced.
Day in and day out,
I performed the fabricated ritual of necessity
that I called my life,
while dwelling on the displeasure that I had decorated
as best I could,
that I might merely survive
to do it again...
tomorrow.

At first, I found myself optimistic
and every time I would spot a beacon of light,
I hoped that it would be the one
that I had been anticipating
for as long as I could remember.

I prayed that God
had sent someone on a mission to find me,
to take me away from my solitude.
I prayed that they would not pass
as millions of others had
on every prior evening.

To my dismay, however,
most of them did pass,
and even more distressing
was the fact that of the few
that happened to wash ashore,
they all still lacked the provisions needed
to get me to leave
my prison of paradise.

The best of them offered to share their own coconuts;

Others offered only to share the ones
already in my possession.

The worst swiped from my reserve
simply to add to their own supply.

In time, my optimism for rescue
evaporated in the heat
and turned only to effort toward contentment
and complacency.

I began to ignore the lights in the darkness
and went on about my business,
expecting nothing...
jaded by prior shipwrecks and false S.O.S signals...
refusing to go near the water,
for fear of drowning in the murky deep
if forced to walk the plank again
by yet another pirate.

I knew that I no longer
possessed the strength to swim,
but I also knew
that I wasn't ready to die.
So I stayed put.

It was precisely dusk
when you came ashore,
intently,
with a look of exploration about you.

I must admit that
I was quite taken,
though I ignored your invitations
for quite some time,
while I likened your ship
to the ships that I'd made the mistake
of boarding long ago.

But then you told me a story,

                                        my story,

set in a different time and place...
with a different

                                        "me"...

and suddenly,
I found myself putting on shoes
that I hadn't a need for in years.

The prospect of coming aboard that evening
got me to admit,
aloud,

      how much I hated dining on coconuts in isolation.

And I thought to myself...

that if I could leave this island
just one more time,
then maybe I could stay gone.

      And maybe

              just maybe...

you could convince me
to say goodbye to this desolate oasis
forever...

      to take your hand...

           and go sailing again.

Every broken ending
is a chance
for a new beginning.

It just depends
on what you decide to do
with the pieces.

Me: He said he was "all in." I just don't know how he could do this to me.

Him: Sweetheart, sometimes people are just shitty. Come on... Do you wanna go get a drink?

Me: (Teary-eyed) Do they have wings?

Him: Yeah. I hear they're really good too.

Me: (sniffling) Okay. Let's go.

Him: So, what exactly did he say?

PART 3

GRENADES

He said to her
in an effort to dry her tears
and ease her pain,
knowing that she needed to understand
that while trying to show genuine love to that man,
even though she'd lost,
she was not the loser.

The young man in question had shown his
lack of commitment through his
lack of effort,
presence,
attention,
and conversation...
all of which she'd offered to him freely.

So she'd retreated to her loft
dejected
because he was not satisfied with all the gifts she'd offered,
the essence of her true self...
rejected
because she did not offer them to him with her
head bowed,
or her legs opened.

But here was another to console her...
 to say that

"We're not all that way. Say where and when."

Requesting nothing more than a time and a place,
he dined with her.

And then something happened...
and the world would never be the same again.

———— ◆ ————

"Do you throw grenades?"

It was a valid question.

Self-sabotage is common
among the "spinster" women of the world...
girls thinking that
love has to end badly,
so they break their own hearts
before boys can do it for them.

All of the reasons for her singleness
didn't add up to him,
and quite frankly,
his didn't make sense to her either.

"I don't throw grenades.
I don't get far enough into the relationship to do that."

Then followed the reasons and situations...
a few stories.

But the full explanation came
when the last of the crowd dissipated
and she told him
that there was a special part of herself
that she would give
to one man
and one man only.

He had no idea
that she was reluctant to reveal this to him
for fear of hearing
what she had always heard...
that her decision was the problem.

She had no idea
that he would find her decision admirable,
and that he would say to her,

"You're doing EVERYTHING right...
Don't change a thing."

She stood dumbfounded...
thinking to herself
the very question that she would ask him
later over dinner,

"What kind of woman would let you go?"

... and then came his tale.

She kept waiting for something outlandish, some
"red flag",
but none appeared.

Someone had broken his heart.

His marriage had failed.

And as he sat across from her,
she made the choice that
if this was her chance
to be with him,
she would try.

She had never really committed before, but
this time,
she would.

She wanted to.
He was worth it.
And with that decision,

something happened,
and the world would never be the same again.

— ◆ —

"I'm sorry that I didn't hold you longer..."
he offered timidly
in an accidental text
turned phone call.

"No one has hugged me in a very long time..."

he explained.

"I just want my students to care..."
said she.

"I stutter..."

he offered.

"I want so many things..."
she agonized.

"Haight blue..."

he quipped.

"The eyeshadow?"
she asked.

"Slow dances, and beauty..."
"Did you twirl her to see her panties?"

They laughed.

"I appreciate pretty..."

he said.

"Salsa, musicality, rhythm and sensuality..."
she went on.

"Boats and sunrises... a symphony of curves and lines..."

And there it was.
She didn't know what,
but it was there.

There, pacing through her living room,
heart pounding
and holding her breath as she
offered him bits of herself
in exchange for
the pieces of him,

something happened... and the world would never be the
same again.

———— ◆ ————

"You have no idea how nervous I am..."

He whispered shyly
as they were surrounded
by the miniature multitude.

Denying the obvious was no longer an option,
and if it was,
he was choosing to confirm his suspicions
rather than dwell in quandary.

They knew full well that once admitted,

this secret

would demand an action of some sort

from the both of them.

She was barely breathing when his question came.

Still she answered it with a timid,

yet whole-hearted

"Yes."

She'd always feared that question,

but from him,

those words inspired a kind of

bravery,

a desire

that she had never felt before.

He

left to take care of his business,

as she

sat there trying to wrap her mind around the fact that

she had a "date."

Scared to death
and simultaneously floating on air,
she put on her comfortable boots,
and prepared to roam into
what was for her,
uncharted territory.

But when she saw his smile
as she stepped out of the car,

something happened...
and the world would never be the same again.

————— ◆ —————

"I like the three buttons on your jeans..."

He told her as they stood on the
bridge, under the bridge.

The columns of the overpass looked to her like
concrete tree trunks
amidst the actual foliage.

She couldn't help but notice just how
perfect the scene was
for the two of them... how
different they saw it, yet how
beautiful they both thought it was.

She couldn't help but consider how
it had been seven years
since her heart fluttered
like it did that afternoon
every single time he
had grabbed her hand,
three in total,
and led her down the trail...
or he'd stopped and
held her, twice,
kissing her,
once
on the cheek.

She couldn't help but consider how
on this,
the very first day of
the eighth year,
the number of new beginnings,
she was standing there
next to him.

And she couldn't help but wonder if
he'd had as wonderful a time as she...
If he'd ever ask her
to go walking with him again.

The silent three hour frenzy in her mind
finally subsided as night fell
and there,
in front of the concrete forest,
he kissed her,
held her,
and kissed her again.
And in that moment she knew,

that something happened...
and the world would never be the same again.

———— ◆ ————

He told her that evening
as they sat on the couch,
a ritual
that would prove to be most satisfying
in the coming months.

She would lay in his arm
and he would talk, the way
she'd never heard him talk, the way
she would never hear him talk,
if she did not make her nest
 upon his shoulder.

Finally,
revealing a few of his more
delicate layers
located beneath the tougher exterior ones,
this self-proclaimed "onion" of a man
unfolded a little.

The conversation,
her favorite part of being with him,
made its way through
meals...

                                            people...
            places...
                              memories...
and decisions.

At times the topics collided like
the time he introduced her to the
loves of his life,
and she got to see him
reflected within them...
to have his face mirrored back at her
two more times,
and she loved it.

Then there were the memories of
his former lives, of
all the things home had meant to him, of
the things that he loved to do
that she had never done, but
wanted to try,
just to experience him in his natural habitat.

They walked the tightrope between
each other's worlds,
with talk of
dancing and duck hunting...
ballrooms and swamps.

"I want to spend as much time with you as possible..."

It was the most wonderful thing for her to hear.
He "wanted",
and it made her feel
welcomed.
"I'm all in too",
she said,
she thought,
she felt...
but most importantly, she meant.

And after countless obligations,
she would find herself calling him
to ask for a cup of tea
and that warm shoulder
where she would rest for the night.
Every time she would enter,
he would kiss her,
hold her,

and something happened...

and the world would never be the same again.

———— ◆ ————

"Do you have a family song?"

He whispered to her in the darkness

as they laid there,

no space between them,

 warm and comfortable,

"pretzeled" as he liked to call it,

and just feeling

blessed.

"No"

she replied,

and he began to sing to her.

She didn't know the song, but

it was the most beautiful one she'd ever heard.

In between lines, he interjected kisses.

She stroked his hair.

And though they never did the deed, the
intimacy within their joint presence, those
moments repeating night after night,
were more than enough for her to know,
that her love letter was safe.

"I'm not going to hurt you",
he'd said to her after he'd read it.

He then cut off the lights,
and guided her to his shoulder.
And when she chose to believe him,

something happened...
and the world would never be the same again.

———— ◆ ————

"Did that just happen?"

He smiled at her
across the bin of discounted intimate apparel.
Other women in the room
had stopped and stared,
giving second glances to
confirm what they had just witnessed...
a little bit of PDA.

They giggled a little at their audience's surprise,
although they were
a little surprised
at themselves.

For that brief moment,
she had forgotten
that there was anyone else in the store.
It was the perfect moment to
follow up dinner
on a lovely Sunday afternoon
where she had introduced him
to her home away from home.

He had taken the ride with her
just to spend some time with her,
which he had grown accustomed to doing
on occasion,
and those afternoons
seemed to be her favorite,
wandering to hardware stores...

fabric stores...

dinner and concerts...

mornings at grocery stores...

craft stores...

and even meeting her parents.

The intertwining of their everyday lives was
as wonderful
as it was peaceful.

One night,
he leaned over in the front seat
and stared at her in the dark.

"Hey..."

he whispered.

**"I can't believe that I'm making out with
my girlfriend in my dad's truck."**

He could be so adorable at times.

"You wanna call and tell him?"

She smiled.

"No, but you can if you want..."

and he kissed her again.

She giggled,
all the while thinking that
this must be what it's like
to be seventeen.

It was blissful,
and in that bliss she realized,

that something happened...
and the world would never be the same again.

———— ◆ ————

"Thank you for finding your way in..."

He told her quietly
as he held her,
admitting
that he had a tough exterior,
and it was almost impossible
to penetrate.

He had tried
repeatedly
to throw his own grenades
by telling her of all his
flaws,
all the ways that he
judged himself too harshly,
in her eyes.

To her,
he had the power to decide
who he was
and would be
in this relationship.

And now,

he had finally made the decision

 to let her in,

that she might really

know him.

"If I want to have the

relationship that I want with you,

I have to make the decision

to try.

That's what I'm choosing to do

with you..." ,

she told him that Christmas eve.

"Please, don't hurt me..."

he said with tears in his eyes.

She was stunned.

How could he think

that she would ever do that?

Didn't he know

how happy

he made her?

Just remembering
the way that he thought of her,
writing her letters,
designing her a home,
he talked about her presence making him
more of the person
he used to be.

His spark was back.

What he didn't realize was that
he made her
the person
she desired to be as well.

"You're my operational best friend..."

and he was hers.
She had been contemplating
for a while now,
just how much he meant to her.

She wasn't sure exactly...
but whatever it was,
she saw in his eyes
that he felt the same.

She knew that
she could never hurt him
because just being with him,

something happened...
and the world would never be the same again.

— ◆ —

"You're the best..."

He wrapped her in his arms.

"I had never realized how short you are."

She smiled,
thrilled that
he seemed to like his gift.
She had been planning it
for quite some time now, spending
days gathering everything for him, wanting to
let him know that
Valentine's day
never had to be sad again.

On THIS Valentine's day,
somebody loved him.
She knew she couldn't say that;
He wasn't ready to hear it.

He wasn't going to be available on that day,
but she would
find a way to see him anyway.

He had been distant and
a little sad,
but understandably so.
His schedule,
the fear of losing a loved one,
and the pressure that he
seemed to always put on himself,
were not easy things to bear.

She tried to be there for him,
whatever that meant,
but he would never let her.
She tried not to
take it personally.

Maybe this was just his M.O..

He was busy
with every facet of his life,
and she was determined
to not be a bother
while still letting him know that
she cared.

After all,
he had written her a letter
acknowledging his busy schedule, but
promising that he would just
owe her more of himself, that
he would be thinking of her,
letting her know that
she was safe with him.

But his response to her began to change.
It was colder, somehow.

"Do you want me to come over?"
began to be met with,

> **"Whatever you want to do...",**

the gruesome equivalent to
"I don't care."

Still she came and crawled in
next to him.
The room was cold,
as usual,
only tonight,
he did not warm her.

She tried to reach over to him and
remind him that she was there, that
she wanted to be in his arms,
or him in hers, but
he ignored her.

It was the coldest night they'd ever shared.

And there,
in what HE had earlier deemed
"their place",

Something happened...
and the world would never be the same again

—◆—

"We need to talk."

It only took eleven days.

He had
gotten bad news,
become distant,
and now they needed to
"talk".
Those words worried her and
after stopping by to
check on him,
she felt inclined to go back
again.
There he finally told her,

"I can't treat you the way I want to..."

**"There are so many other things
that are more important..."**

"I can't round that corner with you right now..."

"You're a wonderful person..."

"You're friendship came at such a great time..."

Stuff.
Just a bunch of
stuff.

But there was no changing his mind.
No matter how much she felt
he was making a mistake,
there was no reasoning with him.

And then came the heaviness, the
uncontrollable tears, that
feeling of weight in her chest,
a kind of sadness that wouldn't even let her
fake happiness.

It was brutal
and it stayed.

Her mind was filled with questions...
"Did I try too hard?"
"Was I around too much?"
"Was I too available?"
"Am I so stupid that I imagined it?"

She thought that she'd made him happy.
...or did she?

*"Was I his mid-life crisis and now
he's done with me?"*
Perhaps the most hurtful explanation
could have been that
he used her to lift his sadness, and
now he was sick of her.

But the biggest question was,
"Why?"
Why did he
make her love him and then just
walk away? If he
didn't really want to be with her, if he
didn't know that he really could, then
he never should have
said the things he'd said,
touched her the way he did,
made a space for her in his life,
and his home
the way he did,
or make all those plans
that they'd never fulfill, because
every good memory
was now painted
in a different light.

It was... cruel.

But the most painful moment came when she
went to collect the remnants
of her things
and he'd already
packed them up,
along with the things she'd given him
not two weeks ago.

She looked at the box sitting there...
the box
she'd went in search of because
she couldn't find something that
would fit all that she wanted
to give to him.
There,
she realized that he
really wanted her gone.

She was being discarded.

And as she stood at her car door,
angry and hurt beyond belief,
breaking,

something happened...
and the world would never be the same again.

———— ◆ ————

"It just seemed like a fantasy."

He said while talking to a mutual friend, and
she wondered
just what that meant.

She couldn't grasp why anyone would
want to end their fantasy.
She'd been
praying for hers for so long that
she was convinced that if ever she did find
her fantasy,
she would do her best to be
his,
to make it last
for as long as possible.

When she asked,
she could tell that he was
sick of the conversation.

Obviously, he was just
ready to be done with it, or
maybe with her.

She'd called him earlier
to tell him that
she didn't hate him, that
she was disappointed, that
she wanted to be friends,
knowing full well that his version of a
"friend"
was someone that
he could take care of, someone
who needed him,
while her version of a
"friend"
was a person that
chose to share the experiences of life
with another.

He would not choose to share with her anymore.
He wouldn't come visit;
He'd kicked her out,
but still she tried.

She tried to stop hurting and
see his point of view.

She believed him when he said that

he didn't mean to hurt her,

but he'd fully committed to the action,

nonetheless,

and he'd done a stellar job.

So what now?

"I'm not going to hurt you..."

"Please don't hurt me..."

Everyday lies echoed in her head,

and she felt like a fool.

Who's hurting who now?

but then something happened...

and the world would never be the same again.

———— ✦ ————

"I couldn't give you what you wanted"

She'd been hovering between hurt
and anger,
wondering if she was mad at him or
at being single again,
at losing him or
being discarded yet again,
when she received the news
that rendered it all
irrelevant.

That Saturday afternoon
she received the email,
pulled into a gas station,
and expressed her condolences.

The thought of him hurting
suddenly reminded her that
as hurt and angry as she was,
nothing mattered right now except
the person she loved.

And she did love him... still.

She told him she would stay away,
but it was now her turn
to break a promise,
and she appeared at his door.

She had also promised herself that
she would never go back to his home, as
getting kicked out
can have that effect on a person.
But it didn't matter anymore.

She listened to him reminisce
and was relieved to see that
he was okay.
They made their way outside and
he told her that
he just couldn't give her
the long-term relationship
that he thought she wanted.

What he meant is that
he wouldn't
if that's what she wanted from him.

He never asked her though.
He just assumed that's where she was heading,
but she found it ironic that
she wasn't even sure what she wanted,
marriage or otherwise.

She had met him, and only realized that
all she really wanted was
for her life to be like it was
for the two and a half months that they were
together...
every single day.

**"I know, I know... and thank you.
I have a list of people to call if I need anything,"**

he said to her
as she hugged him
at the church after the service.
To her, that was code for
"I won't be calling you."

His friends and family kept telling her to
"Take care of him",
but she could only feign a smile and respond,
"He won't let me."

She knew he wouldn't.
She would just be there, as always.
That was all she could do.
And then his question came back to her...

"Do you throw grenades?"

And as quickly as the question came to her,
so did the answer...

"No... but, you do...

And then something happens... and the world is never the same
again."

———— ✦ ———— ✦ ———— ✦ ————

My List... age 28... edit #11

What I want in a guy...
- have green eyes/brown hair
- be taller **than me**
- ~~play guitar~~ be a ~~musician~~ musically inclined
- be a Christian + respectful of other's beliefs
- wants ~~[a lot] of~~ kids **with me**
- currently have no ~~kids~~ more than 2 kids
- have a college degree   *has a good relationship
- be really smart   with his ex*
- ~~dress well~~
- be faithful to me
- dance salsa **or is willing to learn**
- be confident
- be charismatic **but also genuinely kind**
- have a beard ~~...?~~ YES TO THE BEARD!!!
- values my opinion
- would (PROUDLY) date a BLACK WOMAN!!!
- wants to spend time with me
- committed to our relationship
- affectionate
- truly appreciates music, beauty, and art
- like to talk and have fun
- be funny

Her: Well, you said you wanted the experience of dating. Now you know what it's like.

Me: Yeah. It sucks.

Her: And yet people still do it... just hoping to get lucky.

Me: Yeah. People are dumb. I was telling that guy about it the other day.

Her: Oh... that "friend" of yours?

Me: Yeah. I was crying, so he asked if I wanted to hang out for a little bit... Got some great wings.

Her: Dumb.

Me: (smiling) Yes. Yes I am.

INVITATION

...oh my god...

There it is.
That glimmer...
that hint that there is...
more.

Standing here,
you're smiling at me,
laughing actually,
and you make me think to myself,...

I love to make people laugh.

Not that
polite little chuckle
that we give when we
try to reinforce the internal walls
that keep what is deep down
on the inside
from manifesting it's presence
on the outside.

No.

Not the
nervously plastered grin we
force when we're
too proud to admit that we're
desperately trying to
maintain composure...

when we really want to
cry...

but everyone's looking.

No.

A REAL laugh,
the kind that hiccups,
climbs,
and fights its way up in spite of
our best efforts.
The kind our pain
can't help but lose to...
every single time.

I think you learn something about a person
when you experience their laughter.

When you hear them laugh,
see them laugh,
you find out how
open they are by how
authentic their laughter is,

                                        or is not....

whether there is release,

                            or restraint.

How long does the smile take
to leave their face?
Is it replaced with
            tension...

                                    ...ease...

                ...or simply...

                                        ...waiting?

Do their eyes sparkle?

                        Or does pain and distress
                                    take over?

There's a moment of
pure exposure, a moment when
you just can't hide,
no matter how hard
you might try.

I discovered something very special
when I first heard you laugh.

It's not buried far beneath your surface, but you
don't really broadcast it to the masses either.
It seems to have remained an
untapped resource.

There's that
spark, that
twinkle in your eyes, that
because of its clandestine coordinates
suddenly became
all the more precious to me.

I smile,
realizing that I can see you
more clearly now,
and it leaves me thinking...

that you're a diamond
in need of
a little polishing and I'm

soooo excited...

much the way a teenage girl is
when she's found
a new favorite pair of jeans.

...The kind that makes you
wonder how you ever survived
without them.
...The kind that make you
look amazing,
feel amazing, because they
get better with a little
wear and tear
here and there, and
after a while...

imagining a brand new pair is
impossible...
                    ...almost criminal...

because the beauty of their
daily battle scars is...
                    character.

Yeah.
That's you.

The shared pleasure of that moment
sends my mind
wandering,
wondering what I would find
if you'd
let me search the property
beyond your gates.

I'm not naïve enough to believe that
there would only be flowers,
long walks,
and moonlight.
I've considered the
possibly rocky terrain,
            jagged cliffs and
                steep hills,
                locations scorching, and
        ever so desolate.

But from that twinkle in your eyes,
I know.

I know that there has to be
an oasis hidden in there...

                        somewhere.

And it will be like
cherry blossoms in D.C.,
                    or
strolling leisurely down the streets of Manhattan...
a little jazz,
some dancing, and
a meal with my best friend.

That twinkle is so intriguing, that
I'll visit you tonight
in my sweetest slumber.
There,
I'll see my hypothesis
put into action,
while being subconsciously informed
the entire time,

                              that this is only
                              my projection of you.

It'll be part fact

                              and part hope,

but then again,

such is faith.

And as I awake,
I'll be jolted back
into my
physical present
realizing that...

I really liked your laugh,
your grin...

and how I long to see you laugh
again,
only this time...

... over dinner, or...

...at a movie...

...walking down the street, or...

...on the couch,...

...closer...

...beside me.

I want to hear it resonate through the
halls of neutral territory, and

                              more private spaces,

in the same manner that it's
resonating in my mind
right now.
I want to see your eyes
twinkle
just inches away from mine,
up close and
personal
because,

I want to know you.

I want to know what gives you
your spark.
              When it gets going, is it a
              slow flicker,
                     or are you dangerous and
                     unpredictable
                         when stoked?

                              Just how hot
                              is your fire?

But most importantly,
Would you be interested
in sharing it...

                                        ...with me?

                    ... 'cause I'd really like that...

So if you'd be so inclined,
sir,
you have my permission.

This is your
invitation
to come warm me up and
burn my walls
down.

Me: So... I'm working on something new...

Her: Okay...?

Me: I sketched a new dress last night.

Her: Oh... really?

Me: Yeah... It's going to be white raw silk with super elaborate beading. You know I like to sparkle like Ariel coming out of the ocean...

Her: So... an evening gown?

Me: My wedding dress.

Her: OH... OKAY...

Me: ... yeah... remember the wing guy?

Her: Of course.

Me: Well... something happened...

PART 4

REIGNITION

They were...
once.
They were young and strong,
brave and beautiful.

They glistened
like the one that bore them,
being as lively
as the fire of the sun
that gave them life.

Stunning,
captivating, and
glorious,
they flew about on a mission
that coincided
with their pure passion...
to glorify the source
of their grandeur,
to pledge their love
to the only being
more beautiful,
more powerful than they,
because there was no other
worthy of such love
and admiration.

But as time wore on, it wore
on her,
wore her down, and
consequently allowed her to only
rent
her joyous existence.

A recurring tax of her tears
had been required,
as it has always been
of all who dare smile,
but those tears
would ultimately
drench her flaming garb.

He was used to soaring
but suddenly,
he found himself
crash-landed,
stranded in desolation,
suffocating
in a cloud of his own smoke...
the product
of his now burning flesh.

He was being consumed.

She stumbled upon him,

disillusioned by his
disenfranchisement,
by promises un-kept,
the indelible scars
cruelly carved
into a heart
sentenced to continue beating.

His feebleness was evident,
encapsulated by
frustration,
the silent mayhem of his mind,
where no peace
was to be found.

He scurried about his affairs
now burnt, but
determined to camouflage his
singed foliage,
and in chameleon-like fashion
he became one
with the lackluster blue-grey
of his surroundings.

There, he saw her and

leant his ear

to share the load of her pain.

He learned that she,

too,

had been embittered, seeking her

vision

in the present

only to constantly relive

her past,

and conclude that her

vision

may have proven itself

to be...

only that.

She had grown exhausted,
hearing voices
once inaudible,
vocal hallucinations, as they
drowned out
all those familiar.

She became blinded
by the tears...
tears that distorted
any semblance of her former self...
tears that soaked her.

She wallowed in her agony,

                                        and he watched.

She had not known him,

before
when like the sun,
he was warm,
bright,
majestic,
so brilliant that he could only be contained
by the one who gave him
his fervor.

But when his time came,
try though he might to conceal it,
she saw the
flame in his eyes, and that
blue blaze
warmed her heart,
renewing hope
for a flame
of her own.

She wished that he had known her
before
when she was
beautiful,
commanding,
strong,
enlightened and insightful...
a time when she
carried with her a spirit,
as she flew,
that could only be indicative of
her creator;
He was her refresher
and source.

But when her time came,
though she had become
quite weary,
almost instinctually,
she returned again to her casing
to emerge
a goddess
on the wings of the wind,
receiving beauty
for her ashes.

It had happened to her
once before.

In the mundane reoccurrences of her
day-to-day,
it had begun.
It hurt terribly
at first,
so much so that she often
cried out in pain...

Pain that ranged from
slight discomfort, to the
burning of the areas that were
already raw from the beating...

Pain that made her
beg the sun for
mercy,
or death.

But soon the flames overtook her,
consuming everything
that she had been, that
she had experienced,
including the pain,
until there was
nothing left but the
charred dust
from whence she had come.

She was grateful to the sun
for
rescuing her from herself,
for
requiring nothing more of her,

because she had…

…no fight left…

…no flight left…

…nothing…

…left.

She felt a sense of peace
as she breathed her last sigh of relief,
realizing that
she
had finally been permitted to perish.

But when the blaze died down,
she awoke
surrounded by dust.
A familiar figure
returned her gaze in the river and she
saw for the first time
in a long time,
the one she remembered,
the one she'd
always been.

She arose
a picturesque replica
of her former self,
and she knew where she had to go.

She found him,

       seething with frustration

        in the sunlight.

She knew now that she had been

sent

to remind him of beauty

once again.

        He admired her

       for just a moment

     before returning to his original state

         of disdain

      for his circumstances.

She watched him

       flail about in anger as

        he barked at her,

      "It's not fair."

Then quietly,
in consolation,
she leaned in
close to him and
whispered,

"But it's necessary."

In stunned silence
he lowered his head
and let it happen.

The inferno consumed him and
though she did not desire to
witness it,
knowing the inevitable outcome
gave her the strength
to do so.

When it was over,
she finally got to
admire him
as the creature that she'd envisioned,
ever since that day
when she'd seen
that fire in his eyes.

He stood before her
and asked,

"How did you know?"

And smiling serenely,
she responded,

"Because the sun revealed it to me."

He smiled.

Together,
they took to the sky
to glorify their beloved creator
once again,
now understanding the
necessity
of their pain
and their ashes.

After having resolved
to perish,

they soared...

flourished...

donning sparkling feathers
ablaze with passion.

And there,
in all their majesty,
they became
once again.

My List... age 29... edit #12

What I ~~NEED~~ in a guy...

~~have green eyes / brown hair~~ doesn't matter.

- be taller **than me**
- ~~play guitar~~ be a ~~musician~~ musically inclined
- be a ~~XXXX~~ + respectful of other's beliefs
- wants ~~XXX of~~ kids **with me**
- currently have (no) ~~kids more than~~ kids *has a good relationship with his ex*
- be really smart + **gainfully employed** ~~does well~~

Loves people, tolerant, and NONJUDGEMENTAL

- be faithful to me
- dance salsa ~~or~~ *is willing to learn*
- be confident
- be charismatic **but also genuinely kind**
- have a beard ~~XX~~ YES TO THE BEARD!!!
- values my opinion
- would PROUDLY date a BLACK WOMAN!!!
- wants to spend time with me
- committed to our relationship
- be sweet and affectionate
- truly appreciates music, beauty, and art
- funny and likes to talk (a good communicator)
- actually WANTS to be in a relationship
    - can and does take care of himself...
        (I'm not expected to mother him)
            - ALWAYS WANTS ME TO BE MYSELF!!!

Him: Baby, it's gonna be okay...

Me: How do you know? After all of this, nothing has changed.

Him: I know. I don't understand it, but you're not alone. We can do this.

Me: I want to leave.

Him: Then let's go...

EVERYDAY

I finally slept,
too accustomed to the weight of waking
and then worrying,
until I could sleep again.

I silently wept,
and my heart could not stop pounding
as I realized again
that waking was the nightmare.

You paced the floor
seeing the world for what it always had been
in my eyes,
just like others did before.

Your pain turns to rage,
feeling powerless to save me
and those you love,
those entrusted in our care.

I'm so tired of being strong…

    …always having to carry on…

   …remembering to stay calm…

    …"Do the right thing… never wrong,"

 …believing it will be okay…

   …giving them grace and choosing to stay…

  …maneuvering obstacles in my way…

…then you open your arms and say…

     We'll be okay.

    We don't have to stay.

     We'll find a way…

   and I love you more and more…

      …everyday.

I stop and ask why,
like a child who's asking mommy
why the pet I loved
is no longer in my arms.

You have no answer.
You're baffled right here with me,
but you assure me
that we won't ever give up.

You say, "Today do not be strong.
I will help you carry on.
It's okay if we're not calm.
That's the right thing... you're not wrong.

But for now, we are okay.
And no, we don't have to stay.
We'll face the whatever comes our way,
And we'll win at the end of the day.

It'll be okay.
It may not be today,
but we'll find a way.
And I love you more and more...

...everyday.

Her: Hey... you okay? You look a little down today.

Me: I'm fine. But lemme ask you a question.

Her: Sure.

Me: How long have you been married?

Her: About 35 years.

Me: ...HOW?!?!?

Her: (Laughing)... I ignore A LOT... and the rest... is compromise.

Me: OH GOD...

PART 5

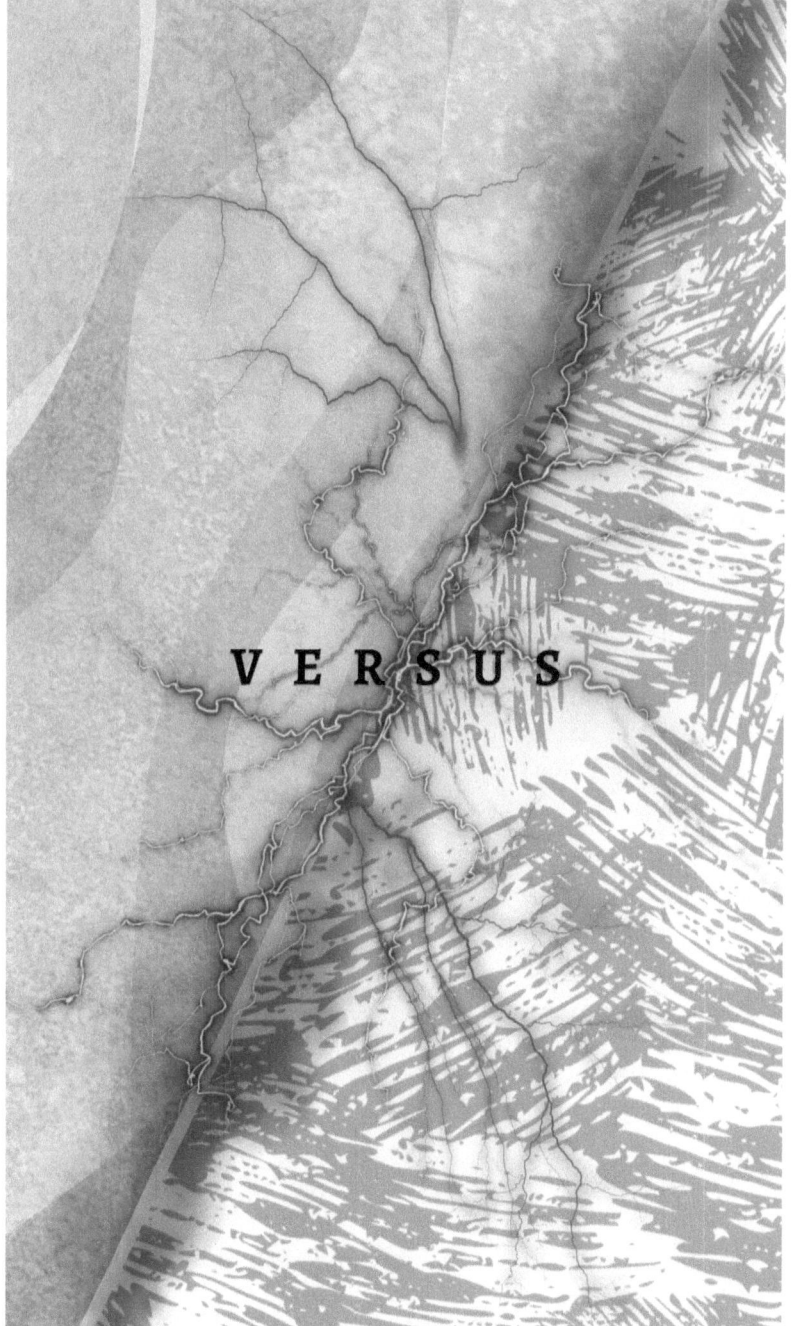

VERSUS

It's over.
I know it is.

For years, I'd searched
high and low
for the perfect alliance,
one that would
strengthen
the value of my dollar, that I could
trade with, that would
aid in my
defense,
both loyally and
strategically...

...because he'd see the vision
that I had
for our empire.

I went about my days
toiling,
busying, and
enriching myself with
experiences and
knowledge...

... and all the while...
I waited for him to come.

And then you came,
more beautiful than I'd ever dreamed, and we
became together, we
built together,
and then...

                              ...all hell broke loose.

---◆---

I'd always dreamt of a life where
every morning
I would awaken,
in the arms of my love
basking in the sunshine that
poured into our bedroom.

We would get dressed and
have breakfast...
together.
We would lovingly
kiss goodbye and
go about our business
for the day.

And then reality set in.

After I constantly wake you with
my snoring...

...and then you
constantly wake me to
tell me to stop snoring...

I then struggle to return to sleep until
my alarm goes off while it's
still dark outside, and I decide to
just get up...
...*sigh*...

...it's fine.

After all,
tired has been our new normal,
for a quite some time now.

I stumble to the bathroom, and
tiptoe
throughout the house
feeding our
very vocal cat, and
changing our
semi-sleeping baby,
all the while
desperately trying not to
disturb anyone...

... least of all,
you.

I used to love listening to
music
while I got ready
every morning.

Now, my heart drops and I
freeze…

whenever I make any noise
above a whisper.

…The man of my dreams
would
be a light sleeper.

But I don't mind.
I recognize that you
demonstrate the patience of a saint
by
running a business,
AND
running after a toddler
simultaneously…
all day long.

While I'm teaching,
your days are filled with
poop smeared walls,
customers at the front door, and
surprise hairball barf
on the floor
in the hallway.

Sometimes,
I miss those days when
we could just
meet after work,
at a restaurant
at the bar or simply
on the couch.

The couch was my favorite.

We'd
watch something funny, something
unserious,
and just...

...enjoy being together.

There was time for
me...
and time for
you.

Now,
"me" time is
whenever I can run to the bathroom, and
"us time"
has become
"family time" so...

...we just make the best of whatever
"time"
we can share.

Knowing this,
you choose wisely to
not bring up the fact that
everything is
everywhere
every time we look around the house to find
anything.

You know
just how busy my days can be.
You understand.

And likewise,
I choose to
avoid noticing that
a sizable portion of this mess
is made up of things that
you never returned to
their original locations, but
left on the counter instead.

I get it.
You have more pressing matters to attend to.

This
lovely extension of grace between us
makes for
a messy house, but
an extremely pleasant existence,
starkly contrasting
the world's chaos, and
air of impending doom.

Our interactions are
delightful, and
filled with affection...

....until I say a thing...

                    ... maybe make an observation...

"Hey... are you okay?"
                              "..."
                                                  "I'm fine."
"Really? ...What's wrong?"
                                        "..."
                                                  "Nothing."

...ahhhh shit.
Here we go.

One minute,
we are doing life together,
cooking dinner,
snuggling, and
talking about our day or
sharing opinions on...

                              ...stuff,

so happy to see
our person...
to feel like
we have backup in this crazy world...

                              ...really cute backup.

In what seems like
the very next breath...

I am lying in bed,
and the passive aggressive attitude that you deny giving me
has ignited a short fuse within the deepest depths of my
soul and now...

I'm in my head,
and...

                              ...I can't sleep.

For the past hour or so,
I've been within earshot of you
pacing around,
mumbling

                                        ...on the porch...

              ...in the den...

                          ... and even in the bathroom
all these complaints
that you said you

                          didn't mean for me to overhear.
Yeah, okay... whatever.

Lying there in bed,
my goal is to
extinguish this internal flame,
or at least contain it for tonight,
lest I let it cause
a true catastrophe.
It's getting late, and
neither of us have the time
nor the energy,
to be the subject of its consumption.

But my resentment toward you
is quickly countered by
my own self doubt,
and I am consumed by that instead.

I find myself contemplating

why I ever thought

that our joyous union could last...

...thinking that surely,

this is it...

...surely,

this is the end of US...

...perhaps my struggle to find love

was a sign

and I ignored it...

...perhaps

I just wasn't built for this

because I obviously suck at it...

...should I just

cut my losses

and set you free?...

...this cannot be normal...

...we've obviously made a huge mistake...

... WHAT THE HELL DID WE DO?!?!?...

I continue to

spiral down this tunnel

at a speed that will soon

break the sound barrier...

...until I hear a sound ...

that brings this train of thought to screeching

halt.

I hear you,
again, in your
not so quiet,
"quiet" voice,
bitching and moaning...
still complaining

about me.

And then I remember that...
YOU'RE
the one giving
ME
the silent treatment...

...being passive aggressive...

... avoiding eye contact...

... giving mysteriously curt responses...

...all while claiming that you're...

"fine".

Blood boiling,
I arise and storm out of the bedroom
toward the porch,
begrudgingly accepting your telepathic invitation to
become tonight's entertainment and
scrimmage for the neighbors.

Seeing you standing in the ring,
I pause.

I can tell that
as a human,
you need validation for your feelings.
As a victim,
you desire contrition from your love.
But as the fierce warrior that you are,
you want sacrificial atonement
for my unspoken sins.
You want blood...

... and as much as I do want to
"just fix it"
so we can rest tonight without any
uncertainty, any
hovering contention between us,
I refuse to back down now.
I will not be bested.

Let's go.

Approaching your sulking form
I realize that my bravado is,
well...

                                    ...just that.
I love you, and
no part of me wishes to lose you...

                                    ...ever.

Tears are now
streaming down my face at the
mere thought of your absence,
but in spite of this
internal admission of vulnerability,
I still meet you in that ring.

Our stubbornness runs deep, my love.

I come out swinging
and deliver the first blow.

"You know that the next time you want to...
You'd better...
because I will not be...
okay?!?!?"

"What are you talking about?
I didn't do that?
You're the one who..."

You bob and weave,
deflecting and denying while I
continue to air my grievances...
the most substantial of them being
that you have no logical reasoning
on which to base yours.

I'm on the offense again.

"I knew something was wrong
when you stopped talking to me.
You HAVE to talk to me.
I can't read your mind."

You stare at me
with both anger
and a little bit of disgust.
It's your look that says

"How dare you blame me,
when you know what you did."

But I don't.

From there,
I weather a steady barrage of blows,
and I struggle to block them,
…ways that I've messed up…
minor accusations for which there really is
no good defense.

But I refuse to let this be a knockout.

You, my love,
are quite the formidable adversary.
You won't go down easily,
but then again,
neither will I.
So at this moment,
self-preservation
is the name of my game.

After you begin to show signs of fatigue, I
state my claims again,
also making many valid points
that you struggle to defend.
Performing similar combinations
to those before,
I take full advantage of the fact
that you are now…
winded.

We go back and forth,
some blows landing
while others miss,
trading punches and
deflecting blame
for what seems like

h
o
u
r
s,

but still, there are no knockouts.

Someone must go down soon.

We continue to
exhaust each other,
by jabbing for a little while longer, until
we're both barely on our feet.

At this point,
all my anger has completely faded, and
in spite of my desire to
defend my honor,
I remember that
resolution
remains the true desire of my heart.

Now, I contemplate declaring it a draw,
to give up and retreat to our corners...

        ...you on the porch and me in bed...

because we are getting nowhere.

But then you perform a combo,
that catches me off guard.

        "No one cares about my feelings.
        I just exist to make everyone else happy..."

I freeze
as a feeling of enlightenment
washes over me.

So that's what this is really about.

It wasn't what you previously cited,
a thoughtless comment made in passing,
but the
presence of deep-seated feelings that you've been
holding onto
for quite awhile...

...at least
judging by the intensity
of tonight's match.

This moment recalls memories, the
stories you've shared with me, the
heartache that you've endured, and the
promise
that you made to yourself
to never let it happen again.

It then occurs to me that you,
also,
have probably been spiraling
for the past hour or so...
just like me.

In your eyes,
you failed at
keeping yourself safe...
yet again.

You went after love and
here you are,
singed,
once again.

I now see that
you're more injured
than agitated, and
this bout
has only further opened
your old wounds.

You've BEEN bleeding,
and now,
so am I.

Sweaty and bruised,
I put my fists down.

I tell you that
what hurt me most was your
cold shoulder.
I can't fix
what I don't know is broken, and
when you say
"nothing is wrong",
you lie to me.

You promised
that you would never
lie to me.

I tell you that

I hate when we do battle,

because

friendly fire is a

waste of

our expensive ammunition...

our time, and

our energy.

> We're on
> each other's team.

I tell you that

I value everything

that you've brought to our partnership...

the intention...

the effort...

the sacrifices.

> I truly desire to
> make you feel as loved
> as you actually are.

And I'm sorry if I haven't

shown you

enough.

Then, I apologize for my spiral, and
I tell you to stop trying to find
subliminal messaging
within the things I say…
Stop trying to infer the
"true meanings"
of my words.

> My goal is never to offend you
> or set you off.
> We've been through this.
> I don't talk in code.

You apologize for
not communicating effectively,
and remind me that
while I can't always fix everything,
you recognize that
some problems aren't mine to fix.

> Regardless,
> we're a package deal, and
> you're not going anywhere.

At last,
We take our gloves off
and step out of the ring,
calling it a draw
after all.

Apologies behind us,
we begin negotiations.
We add new terms to our treaty
and sign,
just in case things ever again
seem as though they are about to
fall apart.

We promise
to come to one another with our needs,
to bring each other aid,
and to remember that we are allies
above all else and
at all times.

We ice our bruises
with apologies, and
bandage our wounds
with kisses
regaling one another
with the many reasons why we call each other
"my beloved",
reminding ourselves of how truly blessed
we are.

We agree that we
chose one another
for all the best reasons
and even in all of this
we regret nothing.

We prolong our
"I love you"s
as if our reconciliation was
just a dream,
as if tomorrow morning,
we could be
at war again.

But once I'm convinced
that you'll still love me
upon daybreak,
I head to bed,
dispensing the last of tonight's tears,
but more in love with you
than ever before.

I finally lie back down
waiting to feel you nudge me
because once again,
I have awoken you
with my snoring.

Then I'll get out of bed
exhausted,
depleted from our match,
to find that you've done the dishes,
but also left random wrappers on the counter.

I'll simply throw them away for you,
as I usually do,
and when you wake
you'll smile,
you'll hold me,
and we'll nurse each other back to health.

And in that instant,
I'll KNOW that everything
about this...

    ...about us...

        ...is just as it should be.

We'll never be over.
We'll just begin again.

My List... age 37...

- Loves people
- tolerant and nonjudgmental
- respectful of other's beliefs
- great father
- really smart + employed
- faithful to me
- confident
- be charismatic but also genuinely kind
- can and does take care of himself...
- wants to spend time with me
- funny and likes to talk (a good communicator)
- wants a committed relationship
- sweet and affectionate
- truly appreciates music, beauty, and art
- musically inclined
- willing to learn salsa
- VALUES MY OPINION
- PROUD TO BE WITH ME
- ALWAYS WANTS ME TO BE MYSELF!!!

BONUS:
- a little taller than me
- has a beard

Him: Mommy, is daddy your best friend?

Me: Yes.

Him: But how? You're nothing alike.

Me: That doesn't matter. He's what I need.

Him: What do you mean???

ALIKE

I know, baby.
We're nothing alike.

We have nothing in common,
but that doesn't matter.

Mommy will
turn the other cheek,
and if you talk to daddy the wrong way,
he might just
rearrange your face.
We're
rock and roll
meets
"Come Thou Fount of Every Blessing".
He's
up all night, while I
can't manage to keep my eyes open
past 9pm.

I strive for a
planned grocery list
for the entire week,
written in order of location in the store
for efficiency's sake,
while he runs
to the gas station
because we just used
our last paper towel and he
needs to clean up a spill.

He's
salmon nigiri
while I'm
a well done steak.
He's the
simplicity of twelve shirts total and three pairs of jeans
with one pair of boots,
while I'm
maximalism at its finest-
three hundred dresses and a
plethora of high heels.

He's

                "I woke up and decided to go fishing today"
and I'm
"Hey... the birthday party is in 4 weeks.

Do you wanna go?"
and then I'm
constantly annoyed with his

"I don't know, we'll see."

Because he's
out of sight, out of mind, meanwhile
I'm
so far in my mind that
sometimes,
I can't see my way out.

But none of those things really matter.
What matters is
who WE are.

Sometimes I'm
"I keep having to pause the video
because you're interrupting it!!!"
but then he's

"I miss you every time you leave,
and I just want to talk to you."

In those moments,
we're
magnets facing the wrong poles…
I desire space…

and he desires connection.

We then might become
pure intentions and,
misunderstood actions…
long and sometimes loud conversations
with an exhausted reconciliation.
But that's okay because…

                        we're also just alike.

We're
respect for your point of view
even when it differs
from mine.
We're
tell me what you need and
we'll figure it out…
and learning to trust your heart
more than I trust my own hurt.

We're
sacrifices for the ones you love…
quitting a job to care for our newborn
or going back to work to provide for us…
whichever makes the most sense
for the family
because there is no pride to be had
when our family is not okay.

We're

daddy making dinner when

mommy doesn't want to cook after a long day…

and mommy yelling "I got it!!!"

when the house reeks because your shit

LITERALLY just hit the fan…

all so daddy can finally play his video game in peace.

We're just alike.

We're

music up too loud

as you bop and

sing along on the couch, while

both of us need the nap

that you refuse to take, but then

manage your tantrums

while wanting to throw tantrums of our own.

We're

shaking our heads and wondering,

"What are we going to do with him?"

and then smiling at each other knowing,

"He's a really great kid."

We're
a combination of "baby, don't cry" and
"It's gonna be alright"...
being held when you get told that
the new baby just
stopped growing...
again...
and realizing that your baby is still
an only child...
being consoled with
"The two of you are all that I need".

And after all of that,
we're,
"I'm too tired... I'll do it in the morning"
being met with a smile
instead of a frown.

We're just alike.

We're made of
"you'll never know if you don't try"
and "you wanna do it, then do it.
It's your life..."
but also "calculate the risk, " and
be smart.

We're made of
equal rights and equal respect
no matter who you are…
admiration for those
who try to make the world a better place
and making every effort
to follow in their footsteps.

We're made of
determination to take up space with
peace, happiness and love,
and the belief that
art and beauty are essential
to a life well lived.

We're just alike.

We're
"I thought you might like this so I got it for you,"
and "I'm making some, would you care for a cup?"…
"I had fun cooking with you"
and "teach me to dance."

We're
a text that simply says "I miss you."

We're
unprompted kisses,
and unsolicited hugs...
Knowing that you don't know what forever holds
but knowing that you want to hold each other
while finding out.

We're
taking the time to tell someone that you love them
everyday
while showing it
and telling them
again...
and again.

So you see, snuggle bunny,
It's not about liking the same things,
Reacting the same way,
Or having the same point of view...

It's about who WE are,
The values we hold dear
and the decision we make to love each other
EVERY. SINGLE. DAY.

We may not be alike
in any of the ways that
don't matter,
When it comes down to it,
We're just alike
in every way that does.

FRAGMENTS

My heart pounds and I'm
lying here
gazing out of my window as
smooth melodies on the radio perfectly compliment the
sheer reverberation of your timbre.

Here.
You are here... and so am I.

The booming bass of your voice,
sends my spine quaking.
I've heard it resonate through the
halls of neutral territory, and
more private spaces.

You call me in their melodies...

              ...on the couch...

      ...closer...

...beside you.

I feel your exhale
disturbing my warm, tender cradle.
It is a sense of ecstasy
that I can barely comprehend.

Where did this begin?
I'd been searching for years.

My memory serves sweet recollections...

    ... smiles...

        ... blushing...

            ... a taste in the darkness at midnight,

and me engulfed in your aura.

Now, you're smiling at me,
and you make me think to myself,

                I really like your laugh,
                   your grin...

and those crystal pools of sky,
that send my heart into flurries
upon each and every meeting with my own.

They are definitely your best feature.

I must admit that
I was quite taken
with that look of exploration about you,
and then you told me a story,
with a different

"me"...

and I thought to myself,

"What kind of woman would let you go?"
...this self-proclaimed "onion" of a man.

I said,

**"I want to spend as much time with you as possible...
This just seems like a fantasy."**

It was blissful.

And I thought,
This must be what it's like
to be seventeen.

Of course,
you had tried
repeatedly
to throw your own grenades,
but…
don't you know
how happy
you make me?
You make me
the person
I desire to be.

"I'm all in."

Because there's that
spark, that
twinkle in your eyes, that
still sends my mind
wondering what I will find
when you
let me search the property
beyond your gates….

Jagged cliffs and
moonlight?
Steep hills or
cherry blossoms in D.C.?

I still want to know what gives you
your spark.

                                    Just how hot
                                      is your fire?

And would you be interested
in sharing it...

                                    ...with me?

            ... 'cause I'd really like that...

You see, as time wears on, it's wears
on us
wears us down, like when
we found ourselves
crash landed
in a cloud of our own smoke.

It hurt terribly at first
but soon the flames overtook us
consuming everything
that we had experienced
including the pain.

Together
we took to the sky
now understanding the
necessity
of our pain
and our ashes.

We became together, we
built together,
and then…

…something happened…

… and all hell broke loose.

Reality set in.
But I didn't mind.
We just made the best of whatever
"time"
we could share, while
reminding ourselves of how truly blessed
we are.

Still,
we regret nothing,
because while we might become
pure intentions and,
misunderstood actions…

We're also
learning to trust your heart
more that I trust my own hurt, and
sacrifices for the ones you love...

We're
art and beauty are essential, and
"He's a really great kid."

We're
It'll be okay.
We'll find a way.
And I love you more and more...

...Everyday.

———————— ◆ ————————

My love,
now I finally see how
the past
has helped to orchestrate our present...

All the words misplaced,
emotions mishandled,
time passed,
and experiences shared,
have brought me
fresh perspective.

I have realized that
who you are is
so much better for me than
anything that I
had ever thought
I wanted.

Instead,
you are everything that I
now know
I really needed.

And as I look forward to writing our future,
I'm grateful
for those fragments of our past,
because now
I see that

they were only...

... glimpses...

...of us.

———— ◆ ————

Dr. Felicia D. Bulgozdy is driven by the belief that artistic expression inspires and cultivates beauty in everyday life.

This belief has manifested in the sharing of her lifelong love of music by teaching elementary music and directing middle school band and chorus in South Carolina public schools for nearly 20 years.

In addition to being a teacher, she loves to perform whenever she has the opportunity: as a member of both contemporary and salsa dance companies, in theatre productions as a singer, dancer, and actress, and in her local choir as a soprano. When she's not in the classroom or on stage, she can be found designing, sewing, and crocheting her own clothing and jewelry, like her very own crocheted wedding dress.

In her downtime, Felicia loves to hang out with her family and friends, and learn to play new instruments. While she loves being on stage, no performance can compare to the impromptu listening parties-turned-dances with her son, as her husband watches and chuckles on the couch.

As she pours her soul into her creative endeavors, she hopes that those endeavors will feed the souls of others, and plant seeds of beauty in their lives.

Feel free to stop by, say "**Hi Felicia!**" and keep in touch at:

www.Feliciad.com
@Hifeliciad on Instagram
@Hifeliciad on TikTok
@Hifeliciad on Facebook